OLIVE PUBLISHING, LLC

All About

Adjectives and

More!!

OVER 1001 ADJECTIVES TO END WRITER'S BLOCK!

Douglas J Boggs

Edited and formatted by Olive Publishing, LLC.

Library of Congress Cataloging-to-Publication Data:
Boggs, Douglas J – All About Adjectives and More! Over 1001 Adjectives to End Writer's Block

Douglas j Boggs - "An_Olive_Publishing, LLC book"
First U.S. Edition 2023
1. Publishing 2. writing 3. 1001 4. adjectives 5. writer's block 6. Writing prompts 7. blogging 8. Title 9. Douglas J Boggs 10. Olive publishing, LLC

ISBN(s) – ebook 978-1-7364715-8-6,
softcover 978-1-7364715-9-3

https://olivepublishingllc.com

29 10 17 28 13 25 21

Other books by Douglas J Boggs:

"Quantum of Justice – The Fraud of
Foreclosure and The Illegal Securitization
of Notes by Wall Street"

"So, You Decided to Write a Book – The
Ultimate Guide to Writing and Publishing
Your Book"

"Don't Forget to Ask"

Look for his highly anticipated
political/thriller "Truth and Consequences"
in 2024.

More at douglasjboggs.substack.com

Contents

Writer's Block

The struggles of dealing with writer's block are very real. There is not a writer in the world that can honestly attest that they have never come across a time when they found themselves at an impasse and were staring at their screen waiting for the words and phrases to come.

Writer's block is an all-too-familiar adversary that plagues writers across the spectrum, from beginners to seasoned professionals. It is a frustrating and debilitating experience, leaving the creative mind seemingly empty and unyielding. Let's take a moment and explore the struggles of dealing with writer's block, its causes, its impact on writers, and various strategies to overcome this creative blockade.

It can be likened to a mysterious fog that descends upon the creative landscape, shrouding ideas and stifling inspiration. It is characterized by a feeling of mental paralysis, a void of words, and a haunting sense of inadequacy. Many writers find themselves staring at a blank page, their thoughts jumbled, and their once-vibrant ideas now eluding them.

The causes of writer's block are multifaceted and vary from writer to writer. Perfectionism, fear of failure, self-doubt, external pressures, burnout, and a lack of inspiration are among the common culprits. The weight of expectations, the fear of producing subpar work, or the relentless pursuit of the elusive "perfect" idea can all contribute to the development of writer's block.

The stress from it can take a profound toll on writers, affecting their confidence, self-esteem, and overall mental well-being. It creates a sense of frustration and guilt, as writers struggle to meet deadlines and fulfill their creative aspirations. For professional writers, this creative drought can be financially detrimental, adding to the stress and anxiety.

While writer's block can be daunting, there are various strategies and techniques that writers can employ to overcome this creative obstacle:

a. Freewriting: Engaging in freewriting allows writers to write without judgment or expectation. The act of putting pen to paper or fingers to keyboard, with no concern for structure or coherence, can help unlock ideas and unblock creative pathways.

b. Setting Realistic Goals: Breaking down the writing process into manageable tasks and setting realistic goals can reduce the overwhelming pressure and give writers a sense of accomplishment with each milestone achieved.

c. Taking Breaks: Stepping away from the writing desk and engaging in other activities can refresh the mind, provide perspective, and offer new sources of inspiration.

d. Seeking Support: Connecting with fellow writers, participating in writing groups, or seeking guidance from mentors can provide invaluable support and encouragement during challenging times.

e. Embracing Imperfection: Understanding that writing is a process and that not every word needs to be perfect from the start can liberate writers from the chains of perfectionism.

f. Trying Different Writing Techniques: Experimenting with different writing techniques, such as brainstorming, mind mapping, or reverse outlining, can spark creativity and help writers discover new angles for their work.

Dealing with writer's block is a universal struggle that every writer encounters at some point in their creative journey. By understanding its nature, identifying its causes, and employing various strategies to overcome it, writers can navigate through this creative hurdle. Writer's block is not an indication of a lack of talent but rather a reminder of the complexities of the creative process. Embracing the challenges and learning to overcome writer's block can lead to personal growth and richer, more profound writing.

I have been writing all my life and have written and published numerous books, stories, poems, song lyrics, articles, blog posts, scripts and more. Despite this I can still find myself up against the white screen or staring at a blank page simply holding my pen or pencil waiting for words to expose themselves to me. Over time, I have developed and used the tools included in this book to help me work through those moments of struggle and frustration and to reduce the stresses associated with writer's block.

180 Writing Prompts

1. Is it for societies' benefit that actors or athletes speak out on social and/or political issues?

2. Is it best if all young people learn how to invest in the stock market?

3. Would it be beneficial if society ended the practice of tipping?

4. List the greatest songs of all time?

5. What are your thoughts about "cancel culture"?

6. Would it be better if there were special separate social media Apps for children?

7. When is it ever OK to be a snitch?

8. Is it OK for a corporation to take a political stance?

9. What are some benefits of Reality TV to our society?

10. Should our schools provide feminine products to their students?

11. Do you think your generation is doing anything to help strengthen our democracy?

12. Do you think the death penalty should be abolished?

13. What is the worst toy on the market ever?

14. Should identification documents offer more gender options?

15. How much has your community changed since George Floyd's death?

16. Can empathy be taught, and should schools promote it to help us understand each other's pain?

17. Should schools or employers dictate how people wear their hair?

20. Should schools named after historical figures with ties to racism, sexism, or slavery be renamed?

21. How should schools hold students accountable for hurting others?

22. What ideas do you have to enhance your favorite sport?

23. Do presidential debates truly benefit voters, or should they be eliminated?

24. Is the Electoral College problematic, and does it need reform?

25. How important is it to you who sits on the Supreme Court? Should it matter?

26. Should museums return looted artifacts to their countries of origin?

28. Should teachers be allowed to wear political symbols?

29. Do you believe people have become too complacent about COVID-19?

30. Who should be the Person of the Year for 2020, in your opinion?

31. How should racial slurs in literature be addressed in the classroom?

32. Should snow days still be observed?

33. What are your reactions to the storming of the Capitol by a Pro-Trump mob?

34. What are your thoughts on tech companies blocking President Trump?

35. If you were a member of Congress, would you vote to impeach President Trump?

36. As the new president, what would be your first priority?

37. Who were you hoping would win the 2020 presidential election?

38. Should media literacy be a mandatory course in school?

39. What are your reactions to the results of the 2020 election, and what should happen next?

40. How should we remember the problematic actions of the nation's founders?

41. How should leaders decide what stays open and what closes during a surge in coronavirus cases?

42. What is your reaction to the inauguration of Joe Biden and Kamala Harris?

43. How concerned should we be about screen time during the pandemic?

44. Should schools be able to discipline students for their social media posts?

45. What art, culture, and technology flopped in 2020?

46. What are your feelings about censored music?

47. Why do you think "Driver's License" became such a hit?

48. How close are we to achieving Justice Ginsburg's goal of gender equality?

49. How well do you think our leaders responded to the coronavirus crisis?

50. To what extent is the legacy of slavery and racism still present in America in 2020?

51. How can we reimagine schools to ensure all students receive a quality education?

52. How concerned are you about the integrity of the 2020 election?

53. What issues in this election season matter the most to you?

54. Is summer school an effective way to make up for lost learning?

55. What is your reaction to the Senate's acquittal of former President Trump?

56. Should we have age restrictions for our federal legislators?

57. How should we balance safety and urgency in developing a COVID-19 vaccine?

58. What are your reactions to Oprah's interview with Harry and Meghan?

59. Should the government provide a guaranteed income for families with children?

60. Should there be more public restrooms available?

61. Should high school-age basketball players be permitted to get paid?

62. Should team sports take place this year?

63. Who were the best musical artists in the past year, and what were the best songs?

64. Should student debt be canceled?

65. How closely should actors' identities match the roles they play?

66. Should white writers translate a black author's work?

67. Would you consider buying an NFT (non-fungible token)?

68. Should kids still learn to tell time?

69. Should financial literacy be taught in all schools?

70. What is your reaction to the verdict in the Derek Chauvin trial?

71. What is the best way to stop abusive language online?

72. What are the underlying systems that hold society together?

73. What grade would you give President Biden on his first 100 days?

74. Should high schools publish their annual college lists?

75. Are CEOs paid too much?

76. Should we rethink Thanksgiving?

77. What is the best way to encourage teenagers to get vaccinated?

78. Do you want your parents and grandparents to receive the new coronavirus vaccine?

79. What is your reaction to new guidelines that loosen mask requirements?

80. Who should be honored on our money?

81. Is your school's dress code outdated?

82. Does everyone have a responsibility to vote?

83. How is your generation influencing politics?

Questions for Creative and Personal Writing to Eliminate Writer's Block

84. What does your unique style say about you?

85. How do you spend your downtime?

86. Would you want to live to 200 years old?

87. How do you connect with your heritage?

88. What do you believe are the secrets to happiness?

89. Are you a sneakerhead?

90. How have mentors played a role in your life?

91. If you could create a podcast, what would it be about?

92. Have you ever felt pressured to "sell your pain"?

93. Do you think you make environmentally friendly choices?

94. What does TikTok mean to you?

95. Do your parents tend to overpraise you?

96. Would you like to travel in space?

97. Do you feel like you are friends with celebrities or influencers you follow online?

98. Would you be open to eating food grown in a lab?

99. What makes you cringe?

100. What type of volunteer work would you most like to do?

101. How do you respond when people ask, "Where are you from?"

102. Have you ever felt uncomfortable with a school assignment or activity?

103. How does your identity influence your political beliefs and values?

104. Do you identify more as an orchid, a tulip, or a dandelion?

105. Have you been finding it challenging to maintain friendships recently?

106. How is your mental health currently?

107. Do you enjoy writing or receiving letters?

108. What has television taught you about social class?

109. Are you easily distracted?

110. Which objects bring you comfort?

111. What is your favorite memory of PBS?

112. Have you ever been embarrassed by your parents?

113. How are you dealing with pandemic fatigue?

114. Have you ever worried about making a good first impression?

115. What would you like your parents to understand about being a teenager during the pandemic?

116. How have you collaborated with others from a distance during the pandemic?

117. How important is it for you to share similar political beliefs with your family and friends?

118. How are you feeling about winter this year?

119. Which celebrity performer would you like to challenge to a friendly competition?

120. How mentally resilient do you consider yourself to be?

121. What smells trigger powerful memories for you?

122. What are you most thankful for this year?

123. Do you miss hugs?

124. Would you say you are a good conversationalist?

125. What habits have you adopted or left behind in 2020?

126. What were the best art and cultural experiences you had in 2020?

127. How do you feel about wearing masks?

128. What role does religion play in your life?

129. How will you celebrate the holidays this year?

130. What good things happened to you in 2020?

131. What new flavor ideas do you have for your favorite foods?

132. What are your hopes and concerns for the new school year?

133. How has 2020 challenged or changed you?

134. What are your hopes for the coming year?

135. How do you view death?

136. What is your favorite fact you learned in 2020?

137. Which places in the world do you love the most?

138. Have you ever experienced "Impostor Syndrome"?

139. How well do you get along with your siblings?

140. Do you discuss the cost of college with your family?

141. Do you consider your diet to be healthy?

142. How do you feel about mask-slipping?

143. Do you believe in manifesting?

144. How do you express yourself creatively?

145. What are your family's house rules during the COVID crisis?

146. What online communities do you participate in?

147. Have you experienced any embarrassing Zoom mishaps?

148. What does your country's national anthem mean to you?

149. Do sports feel different without spectators in the stands?

150. Would you volunteer for a COVID-19 vaccine trial?

151. What "old" technology do you find fascinating?

152. Have you ever tried to grow something?

153. How has the pandemic changed your relationship with your body?

154. How do you discover new books, music, movies, or TV shows?

155. Are you nervous about returning to normal life?

156. How do you celebrate spring?

157. How do you communicate with people who have differing views?

158. Do you aspire to become a teacher in the future?

159. What "overlooked and underappreciated" things would you recommend to others?

160. Which children's books have had the most significant impact on you?

161. How do you identify your gender?

162. Have you encountered obstacles that have made you feel stuck?

163. What is the code or set of values you live by?

164. Do you think you experienced "learning loss" during the pandemic?

165. What are the most memorable experiences you've had in nature?

166. Do you want to have children someday?

167. What have you learned about friendship this year?

168. What seemingly mundane accomplishments have you achieved?

169. Has a celebrity ever influenced you to take a particular action?

170. How have you marked milestones during the pandemic?

171. How often do you engage with content outside of your comfort zone?

172. Do you believe you are living in a political bubble?

173. How does the weight-loss industry impact your life?

174. What creative projects have you completed this year?

175. How are you feeling right now?

176. What are you grateful for?

177. Is there still a place for marriage proposals in today's society?

178. Is it time for the United States to decriminalize drug possession?

179. How can parents best support a student who is falling behind in school?

180. Should people be required to show proof of vaccination?

The History and Necessity of Adjectives

Adjectives, as an essential part of language, have a rich history that be traced back to the earliest known human communication. These descriptive words play a crucial role in expressing the characteristics, qualities, and attributes of nouns, thus enriching our understanding of the world around us. In this exploration of the history and necessity of adjectives, we will delve into their origins, development, and the vital role they continue to play in language and communication.

The emergence of adjectives can be traced back to the development of language itself. As humans evolved, they needed a way to convey information about their surroundings, including the appearance, size, color, and other defining features of objects and entities. Early languages likely had limited adjectives, focusing primarily on basic physical attributes.

Throughout the evolution of languages, adjectives underwent significant developments. In ancient languages such as Latin and Greek, adjectives were typically inflected to agree with the gender, number, and case of the nouns they modified. These inflections helped to create a more precise and nuanced expression of the noun's characteristics.

During the Middle Ages, with the growth of vernacular languages, adjectives became increasingly important in the written and spoken word. Literary works from this period demonstrate the use of descriptive adjectives to evoke vivid imagery and emotions.

The Renaissance era saw a flourishing of languages and literature, leading to the expansion of adjectives' role in expressing complex ideas and conveying emotions. With the rise of printing, more people gained access to literature, further disseminating the usage of adjectives across different cultures.

Adjectives serve several critical functions in language and communication:

1. Description: Adjectives provide a precise description of nouns, allowing us to distinguish between different objects, places, or individuals. For instance, words like "beautiful," "tall," "sweet," and "ancient" help us envision and understand the world in more detail.

2. Comparison: Comparative and superlative adjectives enable us to make comparisons between different entities, identifying degrees of quality. This comparative aspect is essential for expressing preferences, ranking, and contrast.

3. Emotion and Expression: Adjectives play a significant role in conveying emotions, feelings, and attitudes. They add depth and color to our language, making our expressions more powerful and relatable.

4. Clarity and Precision: Adjectives contribute to the clarity and precision of our communication. They add context and specificity to nouns, helping listeners or readers grasp the intended meaning more effectively.

5. Creativity: Adjectives allow for creativity and artistic expression in writing and speech. Writers and poets use adjectives to paint vivid images, evoke emotions, and create memorable literary experiences.

The history and necessity of adjectives demonstrate their fundamental role in human communication and language development. From the earliest forms of expression to the complexity of modern languages, adjectives have evolved to become indispensable tools for describing, comparing, expressing emotions, and enhancing the richness of communication. As language continues to evolve, adjectives will undoubtedly remain a vital element in our ability to comprehend, connect, and convey the myriad facets of our world.

Descriptive Adjectives

Descriptive adjectives are a vast category of adjectives that depict the characteristics, traits, or qualities of a noun or pronoun. In English, these adjectives are commonly positioned right before the noun they describe. For instance: In the colorful cafeteria, excited children devoured delicious treats.

Examples of descriptive adjectives:

- beautiful, witty, wicked

- confusing, rich, new

- strange, rocky, circular

- helpful, competent, smelly

- stable, grumpy, devoted

- smart, muscular, graceful

- scary, safe, wooden

- sleepy, tardy, hungry

- strange, hopeful, proud

- new, dainty, royal

- arrogant, round, efficient

- youthful, cumbersome, fickle

- mild, expensive, small

- rude, generous, courageous

- zany, thin, round,

- oval, dark, hot

- modern, petite, weary

Comparative Adjectives

Comparative adjectives serve the purpose of comparing two distinct people or things. In English, most comparative adjectives end in -er, while in other cases, they are indicated using "more." For instance: Your sister is more intelligent than mine.

Examples of comparative adjectives:

- better, bigger, older

- angrier, prettier, smarter

- kinder, more determined

- more interesting

Superlative Adjectives

Superlative adjectives are utilized to compare more than two people or things and indicate the most supreme or extreme among them. In English, most superlative adjectives end in -east, while in other cases, they are expressed using "most" or "least." For example: Among all the artists on the planet, I considered her the most creative.

Examples of superlative adjectives:

- best, biggest, oldest

- prettiest, happiest, most striking

Proper Adjectives

Proper adjectives are adjectives derived from proper nouns. For instance, at the grocery store, we purchased Mexican tortillas, German sausage, and French cheese.

Additionally, certain proper adjectives may be based on people and places but might not be capitalized if they are used as more general words, such as "herculean" (which you are likely to encounter in Thesaurus.com).

Examples of proper adjectives:

- Viennese

- Russian

- Orwellian

- Shakespearean

- spartan

- draconian

- titanic

Participial Adjectives

Participial adjectives are adjectives formed from participles, which are words typically ending in — ed or -ing— and originate from verbs. For instance, the students, feeling frightened, hurriedly ran away from the terrifying clown.

Examples of participial adjectives:

- burnt, depressed, surprised

- misunderstood, annoying

- shocking, time-consuming

Distributive Adjectives

Dictionary.com states that distributive adjectives are used to refer to members of a group individually. For example: Both team captains took the time to congratulate every member of the team.

Examples of distributive adjectives:

- each

- either

- neither

- any

Limiting Adjectives

Limiting adjectives are adjectives that restrict a noun or pronoun rather than describe any of its characteristics or qualities. For example: The lakeside had many docks, numerous boats, and ten unique fishing coves.

Examples of limiting adjectives:

- a/an, some, few

- dozen, eight, thousands

Possessive Adjectives

Possessive adjectives are used to express possession or ownership. For example: Everyone brought their own dish, and my mom made her famous punch for our potluck.

Examples of possessive adjectives:

- your

- our

- its

- his

Interrogative Adjectives

Some categories of adjectives are more limited. There are only three interrogative adjectives in English. They are used to asking questions. For example: What is the fastest way to get this done?

The three interrogative adjectives are:

- what

- which

- whose

Demonstrative Adjectives

Demonstrative adjectives are used to express relative positions in space and time. For example: I think that color looks great on you, but this one matches those shoes better.

The four most used demonstrative adjectives in English are:

- this

- that

- these

- those

Adjectives, Synonyms, Antonyms

Adjective - Able

Synonyms - Capable, Efficient Skillful

Antonyms - Unable, Disable, Incapable

Adjective - Abnormal

Synonyms - Unusual, Paranormal, Unnatural

Antonyms - Normal, Ordinary, Usual

Adjective - Academic

Synonyms - Bookish, Scholastic, Academical

Antonyms -Practical, Applied, Effective

Adjective - Adorable

Synonyms - Lovable, Charming, Mellow

Antonyms -Detestable, Loathsome, Despicable

Adjective - Attractive

Synonyms - Striking, Fascinating, Glamorous

Antonyms - Repulsive, Unattractive, Undesirable

Adjective - Attentive

Synonyms - Watchful, Vigilant, Careful

Antonyms - Heedless, Inattentive, Mindless

Adjective – Authentic

Synonyms - Sincere, Genuine, Evidential

Antonyms - Fake, False, Fabrication

Adjective - Bad

Synonyms - Evil, Wicked, Worsened

Antonyms - Good, Honest, Favorable

Adjective - Basic

Synonyms - Primary, Elemental, Fundamental

Antonyms - Incidental, Accessory, Secondary

Adjective - Beautiful

Synonyms - Pretty, Fantastic, Gorgeous

Antonyms - Ugly, Shapeless, Ungraceful

Adjective - Better

Synonyms - Fine, Excellent, Beautiful

Antonyms - Worse, Worsened, Bad

Adjective - Bitter

Synonyms - Sardonic, Nippy, Arrowy

Antonyms - Sweet, Cordial, Sincere

Adjective - Brave

Synonyms - Bold, Courageous, Valiant

Antonyms - Cowardly, Timid, Fearful

Adjective - Bright

Synonyms - Light, Dazzling, Shiny

Antonyms - Dull, Dim, Feeble

Adjective - Brief

Synonyms - Short, Concise, Summary

Antonyms - Lengthy, Lasting, Long

Adjective - Busy

Synonyms - Engaged, Impatient, Devoted

Antonyms - Idle, Lazy, Inactive

Adjective - Calm

Synonyms - Quiet, Peaceful, Restful

Antonyms - Stormy, Blustery, Restless

Adjective - Careful

Synonyms - Cautious, Diligent, Attentive

Antonyms - Careless, Incautious, Frumpish

Adjective - Clean

Synonyms - Dirty, Unclean, Impure

Antonyms - Careless, Incautious, Frumpish

Adjective - Colorful

Synonyms - Splendid, Joyful, Delightful

Antonyms - Colorless, Bleak, Discolored

Adjective - Comfortable

Synonyms - Happy, Blessed, Pleasant

Antonyms - Uneasy, Uncomfortable, Faltering

Adjective - Curious

Synonyms - Strange, Weird, Odd

Antonyms - Incurious, Lacking, Indifferent

Adjective - Dangerous

Synonyms - Risky, Adventurous, Hazardous

Antonyms - Safe, Secure, Immune

Adjective - Delighted

Synonyms - Pleasing, Lovely, Amiable

Antonyms - Tasteless, Vapid, Watery

Adjective - Delicious

Synonyms - Sapid, Savory, Palatable

Antonyms - Tasteless, Insipid, Stale

Adjective - Difficult

Synonyms - Solid, Stubborn, Cumbersome

Antonyms - Easy, Manageable, Subduable

Adjective - Disgusting

Synonyms - Crappy, Nasty, Loathsome

Antonyms - Attractive, Fascinating, Enchanting

Adjective - Dishonest

Synonyms - Corrupt, Fraudulent, Immoral

Antonyms - Honest, Conscientious, Respectable

Adjective - Eager

Synonyms - Excited, Impatient, Anxious

Antonyms - Sedate, Cool, Unimpassioned

Adjective - Efficient

Synonyms - Skilled, Proficient, Diligent

Antonyms - Inefficient, Unskilled, Inexperienced

Adjective - Elaborate

Synonyms - Extended, Expanded, Manifest

Antonyms - Obscure, Vague, Mystical

Adjective - Exotic

Synonyms - External, Foreign, Strange

Antonyms - Ordinary, Familiar, Homely

Adjective - Faithful

Synonyms - Loyal, Trustworthy, Reliable

Antonyms - Unfaithful, Treacherous, Unreliable

Adjective - Famous

Synonyms - Eminent, Renowned, Celebrated

Antonyms - Unknown, Unfamiliar, Obscure

Adjective - Fantastic

Synonyms - Fanciful, Quaint, Gorgeous

Antonyms - Normal, Ordinary, General

Adjective - Fearful

Synonyms - Terrible, Afraid, Frightened

Antonyms - Brave, Courageous, Fearless

Adjective - Frequent

Synonyms - Quick, Rapid, Speedy

Antonyms - Infrequent, Casual, Irregular

Adjective - Generous

Synonyms - Liberal, Bountiful, Magnificent

Antonyms - Ungenerous, Narrow, Grudging

Adjective - Glorious

Synonyms - Sublime, Illustrious, Bright

Antonyms - Inglorious, Foul, Disgraceful

Adjective - Gloomy

Synonyms - Overcast, Dark, Moody

Antonyms - Cheerful, Fadeless, Blithesome

Adjective - Grateful

Synonyms - Thankful, Obliged, Resisted

Antonyms - Ungrateful, Unthankful, Crummy

Adjective - Guilty

Synonyms - Criminal, Sinful, Wicked

Antonyms - Innocent, Transparent, Impeccable

Adjective - Handsome

Synonyms - Generous, Bounteous, Dignified

Antonyms - Ugly, Nasty, Awkward

Adjective - Happy

Synonyms - Glad, Comfortable, Cheerful

Antonyms - Unhappy, Uncomfortable, Miserable

Adjective - Harmful

Synonyms - Injurious, Mischievous, Worsened

Antonyms - Advantageous, Harmless, Innocuous

Adjective - Honorable

Synonyms - Respectable, Reputable, Creditable

Antonyms - Dishonest, Dishonorable Ignominious

Adjective - Honest

Synonyms - Conscientious, Upright, Veridical

Antonyms - Corrupt, Unfair, Deceitful

Adjective - Idealistic

Synonyms - Spiritual, Illusionistic, Theological

Antonyms - Realistic, Objective, Physical

Adjective - Ignorant

Synonyms - Foolish, Unaware, Unknowing

Antonyms - Polite, Gentle, Modest

Adjective - Imaginary

Synonyms - Fabulous, Factitious, Mythical

Antonyms - Real, Actual, Original

Adjective - Immediate

Synonyms - Early, Quick, Adjoining

Antonyms - Slow, Sluggish, Inert

Adjective - Intelligent

Synonyms - Knowledgeable, Intellectual, Rational

Antonyms - Unintelligent, Fool, Deficient

Adjective - Jealous

Synonyms - Intriguing, Malicious, Spiteful

Antonyms - Trustworthy, True, Believable

Adjective - Joyful

Synonyms - Delightful, Pleasant, Gleeful

Antonyms - Sorrowful, Regretful, Oppressive

Adjective - Kind

Synonyms - Compassionate, Merciful, Affectionate

Antonyms - Unkind, Merciless, Inhuman

Adjective - Knowledgeable

Synonyms - Intelligent, Proficient, Knowing

Antonyms - Ignorant, Foolish, Senseless

Adjective - Large

Synonyms - Great, Massive, Big

Antonyms - Little, Small, Tiny

Adjective - Literate

Synonyms - Lettered, Scholar, Learned

Antonyms - Illiterate, Uneducated, Ignorant

Adjective - Lovely

Synonyms - Beautiful, Pleasing, Charming

Antonyms - Unpleasant, Tedious, Worrisome

Adjective - Loyal

Synonyms - Faithful, Dutiful, Devoted

Antonyms - Punic, Disloyal, Perfidious

Adjective - Luxurious

Synonyms - Glamour, Sensual, Delicate

Antonyms - Unpleasant, Meagre, Disagreeable

Adjective - Magical

Synonyms - Enchanting, Bewitching, Alluring

Antonyms - Normal, Common, Ordinary

Adjective - Magnificent

Synonyms - Great, Generous, Extensive

Antonyms - Ungenerous, Narrow, Illiberal

Adjective - Mature

Synonyms - Ripe, Grown, Turned

Antonyms - Immature, Incomplete, Raw

Adjective - Modern

Synonyms - Current, New, Present

Antonyms - Ancient, Old, Primitive

Adjective - Mysterious

Synonyms - Mystical, Secret, Weird

Antonyms - Public, Manifest, Evident

Adjective - Narrow

Synonyms - Confined, Parochial, Slender

Antonyms - Wide, broad, Spacious

Adjective - Natural

Synonyms - Inherent, Inborn, Intrinsic

Antonyms - Artificial, Simulated, Synthetic

Adjective - Necessary

Synonyms - Essential, Obligate, Fundamental

Antonyms - Unnecessary, Wasteful, Inappropriate

Adjective - Obedient

Synonyms - Bound, Liable, Devoted

Antonyms - Disobedient, Unruly, Stubborn

Adjective - Obvious

Synonyms - Evident, Explicit, Vivid

Antonyms - Vague, Dim, Ambiguous

Adjective - Optimistic

Synonyms - Hopeful, Promising, Expectant

Antonyms - Pessimistic, Disappointed, Frustrated

Adjective - Passionate

Synonyms - Sensual, Enthusiastic, Keen

Antonyms - Passionless, Frigid, Impassible

Adjective - Peaceful

Synonyms - Calm, Quiet, Restful

Antonyms - Agitate, Resent, Distress

Adjective - Polite

Synonyms - Gentle, Respectful, Decent

Antonyms - Impolite, Immodest, Vulgar

Adjective - Proud

Synonyms - Arrogant, Haughty, Masterful

Antonyms - Humble, Humiliated, Bent

Adjective - Quick

Synonyms - Fast, Rapid, Urgent

Antonyms - Slow, Sluggish, Logy

Adjective - Quiet

Synonyms - Calm, Cool, Peaceful

Antonyms - Agitate, Active, Noisy

Adjective - Reasonable

Synonyms - Logical, Legitimate, Right

Antonyms - Unreasonable, Illogical, Steep

Adjective - Real

Synonyms - Actual, True, Genuine

Antonyms - Unreal, Mythic, Hollow

Adjective - Remarkable

Synonyms - Extraordinary, Exceptional, Distinct

Antonyms - Ordinary, Natural, Simple

Adjective - Romantic

Synonyms - Emotional, Impulsive, Sentimental

Antonyms - Cautious, Vigilant, Leery

Adjective - Sad

Synonyms - Pathetic, Moody, Miserable

Antonyms - Glad, Pleased, Cheerful

Adjective - Sincere

Synonyms - Cordial, Pure, Sterling

Antonyms - Hypocritical, Insincere, Deceitful

Adjective - Successful

Synonyms - Fruitful, Effectual, Victorious

Antonyms - Unsuccessful, Vain, Failed

Adjective - Sympathetic

Synonyms - Compassionate, Soft, Tender

Antonyms - Unsympathetic, Merciless, Brutal

Adjective - Terrible

Synonyms - Horrible, Outrageous, Frightening

Antonyms - Wonderful, Pleasant, Mild

Adjective - Thankful

Synonyms - Grateful, Obliged, Beholden

Antonyms - Ungrateful, Thankless, Ingrate

Adjective - Thoughtful

Synonyms - Reflective, Contemplative, Meditative

Antonyms - Thoughtless, Hasty, Imprudent

Adjective - Unconscious

Synonyms - Ignorant, Fainted, Uneducated

Antonyms - Conscious, Aware, Animate

Adjective - Unknown

Synonyms - Unfamiliar, Strange, Incognito

Antonyms - Known, Informed, Acquainted

Adjective - Unique

Synonyms - Unparalleled, Supreme, Absolute

Antonyms - Conventional, Usual, Simple

Adjective – Vacant

Synonyms - Empty, Blank, Devoid

Antonyms - Occupied, Seized, Swallowed

Adjective – Victorious

Synonyms - Triumphal, Prevalent, Exultant

Antonyms - Vanquished, Defeated, Subdued

Adjective – Valuable

Synonyms - Expensive, Worthy, Costly

Antonyms - Worthless, Incompetent, Useless

Adjective – Wonderful

Synonyms - Amazing, Surprising, Marvelous

Antonyms - Appalling, Atrocious, Horrendous

Adjective – Wrong

Synonyms - False, Unjust, Deceitful

Antonyms - Right, Just, Correct

Adjective – Young

Synonyms - Newish, Fresh, Modern

Antonyms - Old, Aged, Ancient

Adjective – Zealous

Synonyms - Crazed, Hot, Inclined

Antonyms - Apathetic, Alienate, Aloof

List of Adjectives

Below, you'll find an adjectives list that can serve as the basis for your own list from A to Z.

Here is the useful list of adjectives starting with the letter A:

- Abundant, Accurate, Addicted

- Adorable, Adventurous, Afraid

- Aggressive, Alcoholic, Alert

- Aloof, Ambitious, Ancient

- Angry, Animated, Annoying

- Anxious, Arrogant, Ashamed

- Attractive, Auspicious, Awesome

- Awful, Abactinal, Abandoned

- Abashed, Abatable, Abatic

- Abaxial, Abbatial, Abbreviated

- Abducent, Abducting, Aberrant

- Abeyant, Abhorrent, Abiding

- Abient

Here is the useful list of adjectives starting with the letter B:

- Bad, Bashful, Beautiful

- Belligerent, Beneficial, Best

- Big, Bitter, Bizarre

- Black, Blue, Boring

- Brainy, Bright, Broad

- Broken, Busy, Barren

- Barricaded, Barytic, Basal

- Basaltic, Baseborn, Based

- Baseless, Basic, Bathyal

- Battleful, Battlemented, Batty

- Batwing, Bias

Here is the useful list of adjectives starting with the letter C:

- Calm, Capable, Careful

- Careless, Caring, Cautious

- Charming, Cheap, Cheerful

- Chubby, Clean, Clever

- Clumsy, Cold, Colorful

- Comfortable, Concerned, Confused

- Crowded, Cruel, Curious

- Curly, Cute

Here is the useful list of adjectives starting with the letter D:

- Damaged, Dangerous, Dark

- Deep, Defective, Delicate

- Delicious, Depressed, Determined

- Different, Dirty, Disgusting

- Dry, Dusty, Daft

- Daily, Dainty, Damn

- Damning, Damp, Dampish

- Darkling, Darned, Dauntless

- Daylong

Here is the useful list of adjectives starting with the letter E:

- Early, Educated, Efficient

- Elderly, Elegant, Embarrassed

- Empty, Encouraging, Enthusiastic

- Excellent, Exciting, Expensive

Here is the useful list of adjectives starting with the letter F:

- Fabulous, Fair, Faithful

- Famous, Fancy, Fantastic

- Fast, Fearful, Fearless

- Fertile, Filthy, Foolish

- Forgetful, Friendly, Funny

Here is the useful list of adjectives starting with the letter G:

- Gentle, Glamorous, Glorious

- Gorgeous, Graceful, Grateful

- Great, Greedy, Green

- Generous, Gracious, Genuine

- Grand, Groovy, Gutsy

- Gargantuan, Giddy, Glistening

- Good, Golden, Grouchy

- Grumpy

Here is the useful list of adjectives starting with the letter H:

- Happy, Humble, Handsome

- Helpful, Hilarious, Healthy

- Hardworking, Hopeful, Honest

- Hearty, Harmonious, High-spirited

- Haughty, Hasty, Heavy

- Hot, Horrific, Hypnotic

- Hypersensitive, Hyperactive,

- Happy, Handsome, Harsh

- Healthy, Heavy, Helpful

- Hilarious, Historical, Horrible

- Hot, Huge, Humorous

- Hungry

Here is the useful list of adjectives starting with the letter I:

- Innocent, Inquisitive, Intense

- Impressive, Intelligent, Interesting

- Incredible, Irresistible, Ideal

- Indispensable, Imaginative

- Impartial, Immaculate, Impeccable

- Imperfect, Imposing, Impulsive

- Incomparable, Inconsistent

- Incontrovertible, Ignorant, Illegal

- Imaginary, Impolite, Important

- Impossible

Here is the useful list of adjectives starting with the letter J:

- Jolly, Joyful, Juicy

- Jumpy, Jovial, Jaded

- Jazzy, Jittery, Jocund

- Jumbled, Jarring, Jaunty

- Jingoistic, Jovial, Judicious

- Jumpy, Jovial, Jocose

- Jittery, Joyous

Here is the useful list of adjectives starting with the letter K:

- Kind, Keen, Knowledgeable

- Kinetic, Kooky, Knockout

- Karmic, Kooky, Kaleidoscopic

- Kempt, Kooky, Kooky

- Kittenish, Knotty, Knightly

- Knobby, Knitting, Knockdown

- Knuckleheaded, Knowledgeable

Here is the useful list of adjectives starting with the letter M:

- Magnificent, Majestic, Mysterious

- Moody, Modest, Merry

- Modern, Masculine, Magical

- Melodic, Mischievous, Mindful

- Mighty, Mature, Mythical

- Mellow, Multifaceted, Muscular

- Magnanimous, Memorable, Macho

- Massive, Mean, Messy

Here is the useful list of adjectives starting with the letter N:

- Nice, Neat, Nasty

- Noble, Nurturing, Nervous

- Naughty, Nifty, Nimble

- Natural, Notable, Noisy

- Numerous, Nutritious, Nonchalant

- Nostalgic, Nuclear, Numbing

- Numinous, Nurtured

Here is the useful list of adjectives starting with the letter O:

- Obedient, Obese, Obnoxious

- Old, Overconfident, Optimistic

- Open-minded, Outstanding

- Original, Observant, Obliging

- Odd, Oily, Old-fashioned

- Opaque, Opportunistic, Optimized

- Organic, Ornate, Oscillating

- Outgoing, Overjoyed

- Overwhelming

Here is the useful list of adjectives starting with the letter P:

- Passionate, Patient, Playful

- Pleasant, Positive, Powerful

- Precise, Pretty, Profound

- Proud, Pure, Puzzled

- Peaceful, Pensive, Perky

- Petite, Phenomenal, Plucky

- Polished, Popular, Pink

- Polite, Poor, Precious

Here is the useful list of adjectives starting with the letter Q:

- Quick, Quiet, Qualified

- Quaint, Querulous, Quirky

- Quixotic, Quintessential

- Quivering, Quizzical

Here is the useful list of adjectives starting with the letter R:

- Rapid, Rare, Red, Rude

- Remarkable, Responsible

- Rich, Romantic, Royal

Here is the useful list of adjectives starting with the letter S:

- Scintillating, Secretive, Selfish

- Serious, Sharp, Shiny

- Shocking, Short, Shy

- Silly, Sincere, Skinny

- Slim, Slow, Small

- Soft, Spicy, Spiritual

- Splendid, Strong, Successful

- Sweet

Here is the useful list of adjectives starting with the letter T:

- Talented, Tall, Tense

- Terrible, Terrific, Thick

- Thin, Tiny, Tactful

- Tailor-made, Take-charge

- Tangible, Tasteful, Tasty

- Teachable, Teeming, Tempean

- Temperate, Tenable, Tenacious

- Tender, Tender-hearted

- Terrific, Testimonial, Thankful

- Thankworthy, Therapeutic

- Thorough, Thoughtful

Here is the useful list of adjectives starting with the letter U:

- Ubiquitous, Ugly, Ultimate

- Ultra, Unabashed, Unafraid

- Unappealing, Unassuming

- Unaware, Unbelievable, Unbiased

- Uncommon, Unconditional

- Unconventional, Unctuous

- Undaunted, Understated

- Unequivocal, Unforgettable

- Unhappy, Unique, Untidy

- Upset

Here is the useful list of adjectives starting with the letter V:

- Valiant, Vibrant, Vigorous

- Vivacious, Versatile, Vast

- Vengeful, Venomous, Viable

- Vigilant, Vindictive, Violent

- Virtuous, Vocal, Volatile

- Voluptuous, Voracious

- Vulnerable, Vulgar, Venerated

- Victorious

Here is the useful list of adjectives starting with the letter W:

- Warm, Witty, Wise

- Wonderful, Wondrous

- Wild, Wealthy, Whimsical

- Wavy, Weary, Weak

- Wicked, Well-behaved

- Well-groomed, Well-mannered

- Wholesome, Wide, Willful

- Winsome, Worried

Here is the useful list of adjectives starting with the letter Y:

- Yearning, Yellow, Yielding

- Young, Youthful, Yearly

- Yearlong, Yummy, Yawning

- Yare, Yester, Yestern

- Yielded, Yielding, Yippy

- Yummylicious, Yucky

- Yowling, Yawningly, Yarely

Here is the useful list of adjectives starting with the letter Z:

- Zany, Zappy, Zestful

- Zesty, Zippy, Zen

- Zonal, Zonalized, Zoological

- Zonalistic, Zonked, Zealous

Adjective   Comparative

Adjective	Comparative
Angry	Angrier
Bad	Worse
Big	Bigger
Bitter	Bitterer
Black	Blacker
Bland	Blander
Bloody	Bloodier
Blue	Bluer
Bold	Bolder
Bossy	Bossier
Brave	Braver
Brief	Briefer
Bright	Brighter
Broad	Broader
Busy	Busier
Calm	Calmer
Cheap	Cheaper
Chewy	Chewier
Chubby	Chubbier

Classy	Classier
Clean	Cleaner
Clear	Clearer
Clever	Cleverer
Close	Closer
Cloudy	Cloudier
Clumsy	Clumsier
Coarse	Coarser
Cold	Colder
Cool	Cooler
Crazy	Crazier
Creamy	Creamier
Creepy	Creepier
Crispy	Crispier
Cruel	Crueler
Crunchy	Crunchier
Curly	curlier
Curvy	Curvier
Cute	Cuter
Damp	Damper
Dark	Darker

Deadly	Deadlier
Deep	Deeper
Dense	Denser
Dirty	Dirties
Dry	Drier
Dull	Duller
Dumb	Dumber
Dusty	Dustier
Early	Earlier
Easy	Easier
Faint	Fainter
Fair	Fairer
Fancy	Fancier
Fat	Fatter
Few	Fewer
Fierce	Fiercer
Filthy	Filthier
Fine	Finer
Firm	Firmer
Flaky	Flakier
Flat	Flatter

Fresh	Fresher
Friendly	Friendlier
Full	Fuller
Funny	Funnier
Gentle	Gentler
Hip	Hipper
Hot	Hotter
Humble	Humbler
Hungry	Hungrier
Icy	Icier
Itchy	Itchier
Juicy	Juicier
Kind	Kinder
Large	Larger
Late	Later
Lazy	Lazier
Light	Lighter
Likely	Likelier
Little	littler
Nice	Nicer
Noisy	Noisier

Odd	Odder
Oily	Oilier
Old	Older/Elder
Plain	Plainer
Polite	Politer
Poor	Poorer
Pretty	Prettier
Proud	Prouder
Pure	Purer
Quick	Quicker
Quiet	Quieter
Rare	Rarer
Sincere	Sincerer
Skinny	Skinnier
Sleepy	Sleepier
Slim	Slimmer
Slow	Slower
Small	Smaller
Smart	Smarter
Smelly	Smellier
Smoky	Smokier

Smooth	Smoother
Soft	Softer
Soon	Sooner
Sore	Sorer
Tall	Taller
Tener	Tenderer
Unhappy	Unhappier
Unique	More Unique
Vivid	More Vivid
Vocal	More Vocal
Vast	Vaster
Warm	Warmer
Wise	Wiser
Wild	Wilder
Young	Younger
Yellow	Yellower
Yummy	Yummier
Zany	Zanier
Zesty	Zestier
Zealous	More Zealous